Taxus Baccata

First published 2020 by The Hedgehog Poetry Press

Published in the UK by
The Hedgehog Poetry Press
Coppack House, 5
Churchill Avenue
Clevedon
BS21 6QW

www.hedgehogpress.co.uk

ISBN: 978-1-913499-09-9

9 8 7 6 5 4 3 2 1

A CIP Catalogue record for this book is available from the British Library.

Taxus Baccata

A collection of Nature Poetry

includes poems based on myth, folklore, and legend around trees

by

Patricia M Osborne

In Memory of
my dearest mum,

Lila (1932-2014)

And Sister,

Heather (1956-2009)

Two courageous and inspiring women.

A light went out in my heart when you both left this world.

Contents

MAY BLOOM

Beware the hawthorn,
its white blossom smells of death,
bringing black angels.

MAY TREE

Faye rustles silver translucent wings,
ash blonde ringlets lift
in the breeze. She perches

on a branch. Her lime tutu teases
long slender legs.

Little Daisy tiptoes
under the mass of white.

'Where are you, Faery?
May I have a pretty flower?'

The faery smiles, glides
around the tree,
gently snips a sprig of hawthorn.

'Place this outside your home;
good luck will follow, evil spirits fade.'

Clutching her prize, Daisy skips
away, turns back and waves.

Old Agnes shuffles
across dry pasture. She stops
at the tree.

Faeries hover, whisper warnings.

Behind the tree trunk
imps and elves wait
open-mouthed.

Old Agnes stretches her arm,
tugs at the bough, snatches
a twig.

Faye's face stiffens, lips twitch.
She nods to her faery friends.

A thorn jabs the old woman's palm,
a red pearl drips.
Old Agnes hobbles home.

RITUAL

I
plunge
from the sky
to the open
driveway,
flat
on my back,
wings dry.
Wings limp.

My magpie
family
swarm
from rooftops,
circle my corpse
out of respect.

One
by one
they peck
my carcass,
bid me
goodbye
and leave me sprawled
on the tarmac.

PATRIARCH

Insects and spiders tiptoe
over my peeling bark,

burrow deeper and deeper
into shadows
of salmon-coloured cracks
and crevices.

Up and down my trunk,
squirrels, badgers and bats scurry
using my branches as a trapeze.

Caterpillars forage
on lichen from fungi
stuck to my skin.

On the makeshift bench
lovers cosy
in my hollow girth.

Young lads dig
heels into my grooves.
They climb higher,
my bark bleeds.

When the storm threatens,
schoolgirls scuttle—

swathed

in shelter,   cocooned.

SOULMATES

Last survivors,
Gog and Magog
lean side by side
on Tor Hill's dry plain.

Gnarled trunks,
stretched girths,
cracks and circles.

Branches creak,
royal-yellow
catkins kiss, caress.

Magog, shrunk with age,
hunches, an old woman.

Gog taller, majestic, sways
sideways, brushes
Magog's bough.

Sun burns
strong,
branches
          wilt,
scallop-leaves scorch,
earth   splits.

A feral flame guzzles
Gog's bark.
Skeletal, blistered, bare,
he's grown
his last flower.

Magog stoops
lower, her branches languish,

she wills her earthly
trunk to die

so her   spirit

      may fly with Gog.

LEDA'S RECOMPENSE

Goose-guised,
I soar into the blue,
break free from Zeus.

Relieved from the chase,
breathing freedom,
I glide over sea and land
gaining distance.

Fatigued, my eyes droop,

shortness
of breath
makes me wheeze,

hunger pangs
cramp
my stomach.

My pace relents.

A humming from grey vapours
shatters my solace,

the shape-shifter
seizes my nape in his bill,
lunges at my wings

forcing me to land.

Zeus in the form
of a sacred swan
overpowers me.

Sick in my belly,
panting,
helpless—

He mounts.

Thirty-five days later
my egg hatches.

Recompense—

Helen the Beautiful is born.

STRATFORD MUMS

Scarlet and gold maples wave
either side of slow wrinkled water.
A mother with five murky young
paddles up and down.

She stops, long neck bent
into 'C,' nuzzles
snow plumage
to rub her coat clean.

Head lifted, she stretches
towards puffed clouds,
buckles wide wings, stands
on tiptoe, quivers,

swings backwards,
signals cygnets
to follow in line,
and swims up the Avon.

OAK OF AVALON

Snap.

Branches creak,
foliage rustles.

Sap dries in my bark.

I'm sliced into circles:
King Arthur's Round Table.

Knights sit down,
chew wafer-thin bread,
swill blood-red wine.

I am Sanctuary,

listening to their tales,
plots for battles to win the war.

Morning pinks the sky.
Knights and King Arthur
ride off to Camlann,
leaving me alone.

Stars glimmer,
water ripples,
a barge drifts to shore.

Young Merlin steps onto land,
Arthur's crimson-stained corpse
slumped in his arms.
He sets the King of Camelot down.

I cradle him in my hollow,
on the Isle of Avalon.

SEAGULL SEQUENCE

1.

Wrong Turn

Seagulls flock
in snow coats
above the jewelled lake,

a wrong turn
inland
away from the sea.

High amongst clouds,
formations dance
without sound

flip up and down,
stop, turn around, split,
aim for invasion.

White wings fall
like tissue paper
on rippled waves.

2.

Invasion from Brighton

Gallant geese evacuate,
driven out by snowy invaders,
seagulls squawk to claim their victory.

Mottled mallard and widgeon
scatter to sheltered bays,
concealed from flocks of snow-white birds
that hover above the storm-kissed lake.

Red-beaked moorhens, veiled from view,
bide their time for militant gulls to rocket away
and evacuees return.

3.

Water Harmony

Triumphant geese
return to fold,
wings spread,
joyful gabble.

Yellow croci spring
up in green,
pink camellias cluster
the circle of sun-washed water.

Coots and moorhens
boasting red or white beaks
chug along
creating ripples.

Mallard and widgeon
emerge from hiding,
a pure white
feathered duck in tow.

LADY OF THE WOODS

She stretches towards the stars,
heart-shaped foliage dances,
airy, pendulous branches sway.

Gently I peel away
paper-thin white crusts
patterned with black crevices.

I burn the bark
under moonlight
to keep Isolde warm.

Sapphire flames mesmerise,
crackles soothe.

We inhale timbered scent,
drink clear, sweet sap
and wintergreen tea.

I spread a red sheet
onto the clay ground,

ease Isolde down,
caress her shoulders.

We take our final offering,
the promise of fertility,
gifted by the Lady of the Woods.

THE ENGLISH YEW

Mother Nature had been unkind,
given me a night-time coat,
a gnarly girth.

A faery hovered on my bough,
whispered to the air,
sprinkled me with gold leaf threads.

My heartwood swirled with bliss.

I roused with quivers-
robbers had stripped my branches bare.

The faery cast another spell,
prized my foliage
with pure crystal pointers
sparkling in the sun.

A storm approached, hailstones
attacked me, my gems
                fractured.

The faery circled,
granted me a present
of broad leaves,
glossy and glowing
in the wind.

They blew with the breeze,
drifted in the air.

The fairy waved her wand,
rebirthed my original dress.

She whispered,
Yew are gifted with magic,
Yew wear a coat of emerald gems.

I shook my canopy.

Yew my friend are sacred,
Yew protect the dead,
Yew house living creatures.

My jewels shimmered.

SKY BALLET

Thousands perform
in sequence, chatter,
swirl, change
direction,
triangular wings
beat in unison—

an acro—
            batic mass
elevates,
black dots darken
the sky—

startling scenes belt the blue—

...hearts, balloons
            ...puffs of smoke...

a murmuration of starlings migrate.

MOTHER YEW

High-pitched see-see-sees
sing softly in my crown

A pair of goldcrests
fidget all day
h
ang
ing
upside
d
ow
n
f l i c k i n g   w i n g s
cra
ning
n e c k s

scrutinising stems
in search of food

Fine-ridged toes
c
r
e   e   p

a   l o n g
my arms

G=R=I=P
my pine fingers
prise aphids

C R U N C H

Tiny parents weave

a basket of moss and lichen
glued with threads
~ ~ ~ ~ of ~ ~ ~ ~ spidery ~ ~ ~ silk ~ ~ ~ ~

see-see-seeing   as they work

LIQUID AMBER

Pulham fountain flows,
children clamber
on stained Jersey cows,

finches flit from tree to tree.
ducks dive,
coots and moorhens chug.

Yarn bombs cuddle bark,
kiss orange fiery branches
under liquid amber's umbrella.

WATER STALKER

Like a dancer he unwinds,
stretches his neck upwards
as sun mirrors his shadowed eye.

Under the decayed tree,
the gatecrasher hides, disguised
in his steel grey coat, searching
the shimmering lake.

From left to right, his ashen head
slowly stirs—
he stalks
in silence.

Ready to spear, his pointed beak glistens
in clear view. Innocent prey
continue to play, unaware.

This intruder waits
for the perfect time
to pounce—

DIVINE MARRIAGE

Erected by May Day folk,
a birch pole promises
fertility.

In the light breeze
silk ribbons ripple,
white, green, red.

Colour-catching lovers
weave in circles.

Succumbed by love,
young oak,
Jack-in-the-Green,

takes May Queen, Flora,
goddess of spring,
as his bride.

Linked together with Mother Earth,
Flora digests Jack's sacred seed.

SUNRISE CONCERTANTE

Burnt golden rays break
the night-time sky,
beating on the Ouse's slow crawl.

Air warmed sweet-grasses
fan fragrance into the wind:
marsh marigolds shine.

A blackbird's
chromatic glissando sweeps

towards the riverbank.

Swanking his red tuxedo, a robin
trills to join the recital

as elm silhouettes dance,
watching their mirror image.

The mistle thrush flaunts
his speckled belly. He takes his turn
to chant – introduces

hedge sparrows who chatter,
boast brown suits.

A cadenza call governs the concerto—
plump skylark makes his solo in the skies.

Shades of light peep,
geese chevron across the blue,
noses down, necks stretched, wings

spread wide. Honking their signal sound,
they climb the horizon and sky-fall
on to daylight's iridescent waves.

TAXUS BACCATA

Come to me
with pelvic burn

I will cool you

Come to me

with temple pain

I will soothe you

Come to me

with arthritic limbs

I will ease them

I am your healer

Come to me –

with cancer   I will shrink

your swelling

Come to me –

strip my young shoots

cut the flesh from my berries

collect my needle clippings

I am your healer—

ACKNOWLEDGMENTS

Many thanks to the editors of the following publications in which these poems have previously been published:

May Tree	Reach Magazine IDP (2018)
Soulmates	Reach Magazine IDP (2019)
Leda's Recompense	Reach Magazine IDP (2019)
Stratford Mums	Sarasvati IDP (2017)
Seagull Sequence	Sarasvati IDP (2017) Ingenue Magazine (2019)
Lady of the Woods	Reach Magazine IDP (2018)
Sky Ballet	Sarasvati IDP (2017)
Sunrise Concertante	Sarasvati IDP (2017)

Special thanks to Maureen Cullen, Sheena Bradley, Corinne Lawrence, and Suzi Bamblett, for their continued support and valuable feedback. Gratitude goes to Craig Jordan-Baker at University of Brighton for pushing me to the next level in narrative poetry. Finally, I'd like to thank Mark Davidson at Hedgehog Poetry Press for offering me this publishing opportunity.